Collins

真正

Real Shanghai Mathematics
Practice Book

1.1

少年兒童出版社
Juvenile & Children's Publishing House

世纪出版

MIX
Paper from responsible sources
FSC www.fsc.org FSC™ C007454

This book is produced from independently certified FSC paper to ensure responsible forest management.

For more information visit: www.harpercollins.co.uk/green

William Collins' dream of knowledge for all began with the publication of his first book in 1819. A self-educated mill worker, he not only enriched millions of lives, but also founded a flourishing publishing house. Today, staying true to this spirit, Collins books are packed with inspiration, innovation and practical expertise. They place you at the centre of a world of possibility and give you exactly what you need to explore it.

Collins. Freedom to teach.

Collins
An imprint of HarperCollins*Publishers*
The News Building
1 London Bridge Street
London
SE1 9GF

> **Browse the complete Collins catalogue at**
> **www.collins.co.uk**

Published by arrangement with Shanghai Century Publishing Group Co., Ltd.

10 9 8 7 6 5 4 3 2 1

ISBN 978-0-00-826158-0

The educational materials in this book were compiled in accordance with the course curriculum produced by the Shanghai Schools (Pre-Schools) Curriculum Reform Commission and 'Maths Syllabus for Shanghai Schools (Trial Implementation)' for use in Primary 1 First Term under the nine-year compulsory education system.

These educational materials were compiled by the head of Shanghai Normal University, and reviewed and approved for trial use by Shanghai Schools Educational Materials Review Board.

The writers for this book's educational materials are:

Editor-in-Chief: Huang Jianhong
Guest Writers: Huang Jianhong, Tong Hui, Xu Peijing

British Library Cataloguing in Publication Data
A catalogue record for this publication is available from the British Library.

For the English edition:

Primary Publishing Director: Lee Newman
Primary Publishing Managers: Fiona McGlade, Lizzie Catford
Editorial Project Manager: Mike Appleton
Editorial Manager: Amanda Harman
Editorial Assistant: Holly Blood
Managing Translator: Huang Xingfeng
Translators: Chen Qingqing, Chen Yilin, Huang Chunhua,
Peng Yuyun, Zhu Youqin
Lead Editor: Tanya Solomons
Copyeditor: Joan Miller
Proofreader: Joan Miller, Melanie Thompson
Cover artist: Amparo Barrera
Designer: Ken Vail Graphic Design
Production Controller: Sarah Burke
Printed and bound by CPI Group (UK) Ltd, Croydon CR0 4YY

All images with permission from Shanghai Century Publishing Group.

Contents

Unit One: Numbers from 0 to 10

How many dogs are there altogether?

How many dogs are wearing a bow tie?

How many dogs are not wearing a bow tie?

The table below lists the sections in this unit.

After completing each section, assess your work.

(Use 🙂 if you are satisfied with your progress or 😐 if you are not satisfied.)

Section	Self-assessment
1. Let's sort	
2. Let's count	
3. Ordinal numbers	
4. Let's compare	
5. The number line	

1. Let's sort

Pupil Textbook page 3

1. Sort the objects and discuss your reasons.

I sorted the flags by size.

a.

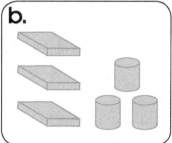

b.

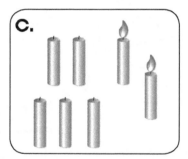

c.

2. Sort and circle (at least one way).

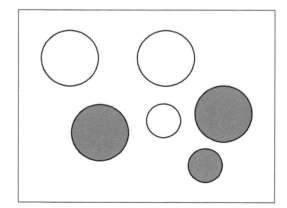

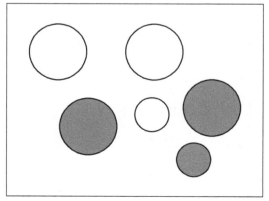

2. Let's count

Pupil Textbook pages 4–7

1. Count, circle and match.

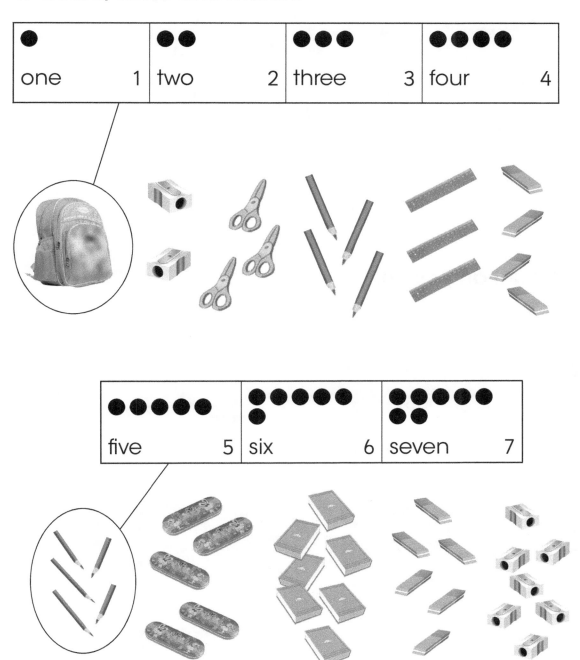

| one | 1 | two | 2 | three | 3 | four | 4 |

| five | 5 | six | 6 | seven | 7 |

| eight   8 | nine   9 | ten   10 |

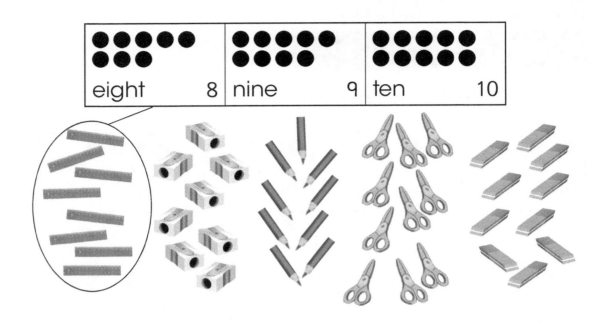

2. Count and circle.

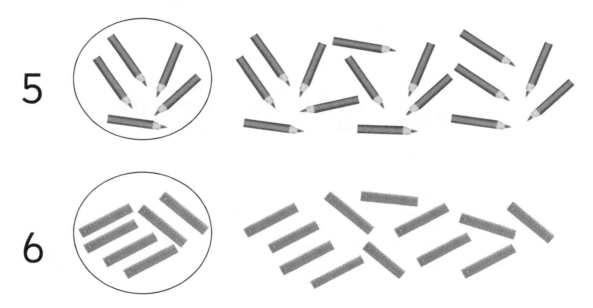

5

6

7

8

9

10

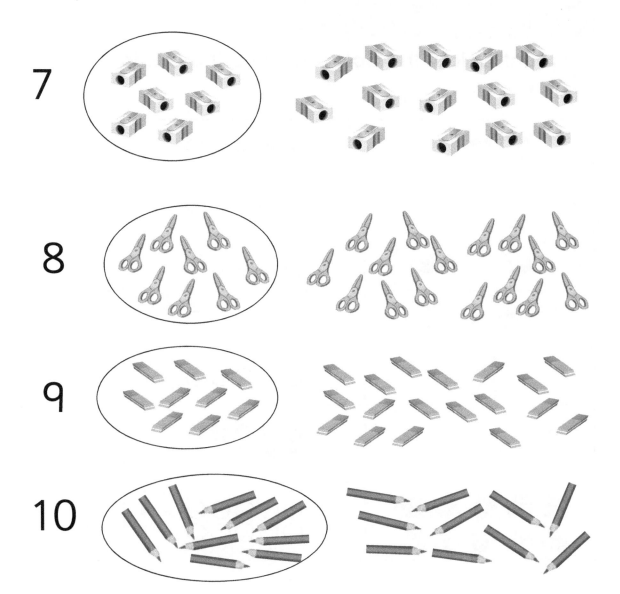

Pupil Textbook pages 8–9

1. Count, colour the dots and write the missing numbers.

ping pong paddles	●●●○○	3
yo-yos	○○○○○	
fire trucks	○○○○○	
soccer balls	○○○○○	
backpack	○○○○○	
pears	●●●●● ●●●○○	8
strawberries	○○○○○ ○○○○○	
apples	○○○○○ ○○○○○	
bananas	○○○○○ ○○○○○	
cherries	○○○○○ ○○○○○	

2. Count and circle.

2

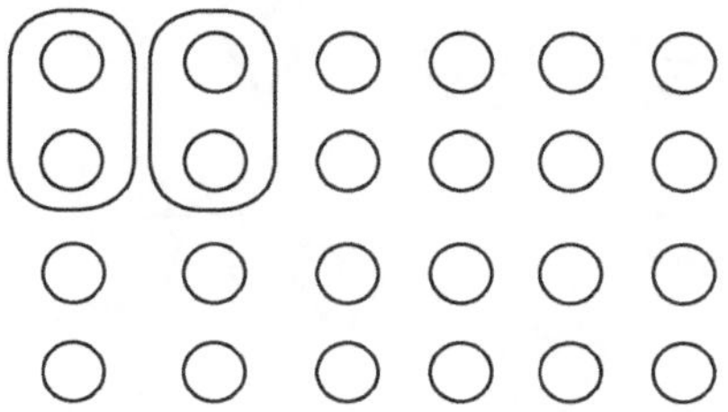

4

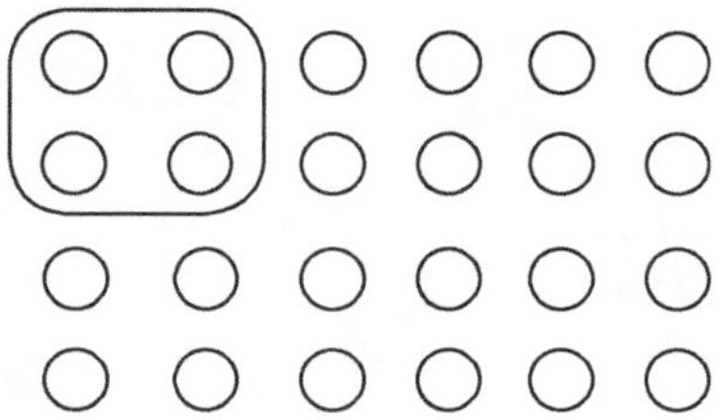

5

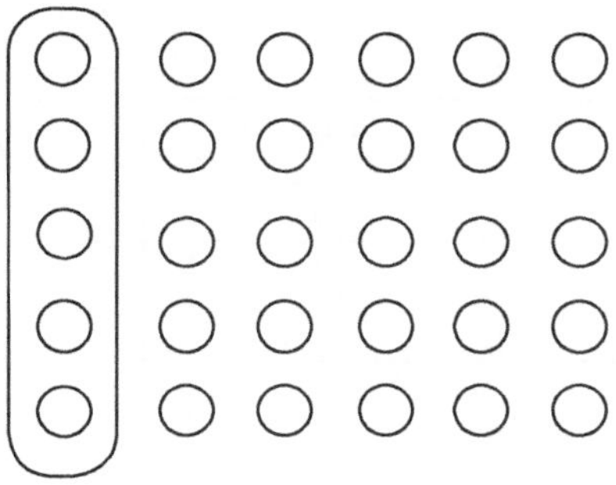

10

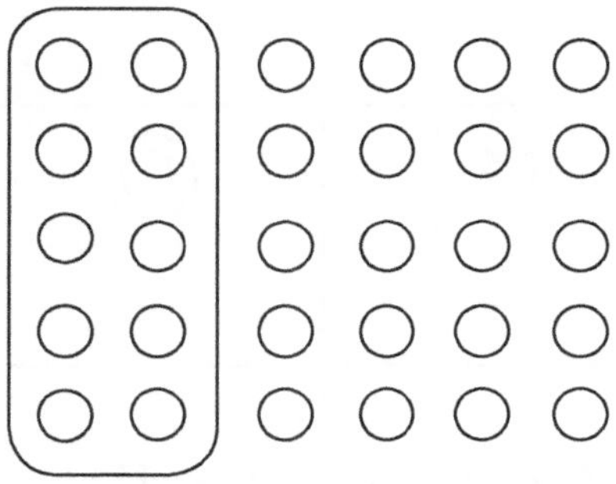

Pupil Textbook page 10

1. Count, and write the missing numbers in the boxes.

☼	◎	☆	♡	☺
7				

2. Count and write.

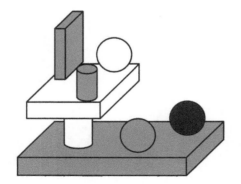

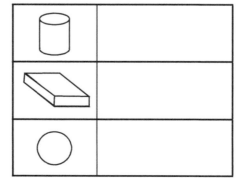

1. Count and circle. (Circle groups of 10 items.)

2. Look at the pictures and fill in the numbers.

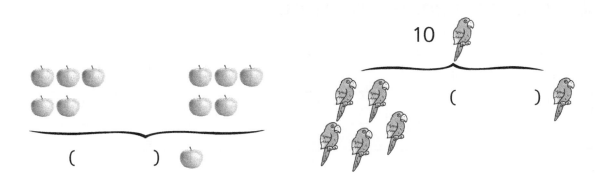

10

(   )

(   )

Pupil Textbook page 13

1. Write the numbers in the boxes.

a. How many carrots are there?

☐ ☐ ☐

b. How many balls are there?

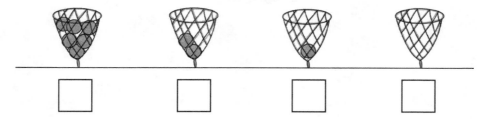

☐ ☐ ☐ ☐

c. How many dots are there?

☐ ☐ ☐ ☐ ☐ ☐

2. Write the numbers in the boxes.

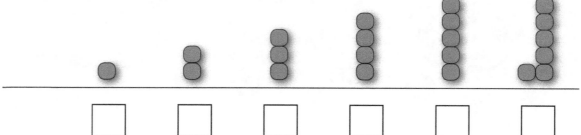

☐ 1 2 ☐ ☐ ☐ 6 ☐ 8 ☐ ☐

1. Count and circle.

a. Circle the birds in groups of 7.

b. Circle the objects in groups of 8.

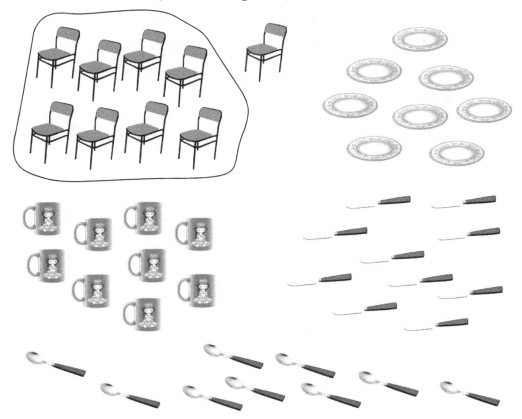

11

c. Circle the flowers in groups of 9.

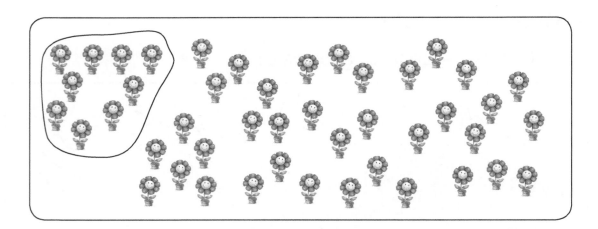

2. Poppy has 7 two-colour counters. One side of each counter is black and the other side is grey. Poppy drops the counters on the ground and counts how many there are of each colour. Her first count is listed in the table. She tries again a few times. Record some different ways the counters could land.

●	○
4	3

3. Ordinal numbers

Pupil Textbook pages 15–16

1. What are their positions?

	second				

2. Count and write your answers in the brackets.

a. There are (   ) and (   ) .

b. There are (   ) pieces of fruit altogether.

c. Counting from the left, is in the (   ) position, and is in the (   ) position.

d. Counting from the right, is in the (   ) position and is in the (   ) position.

3. Count, draw and circle.

a. There are (   ) birds in total.

b. Counting from the left, circle the last 5 birds in this picture.

c. Counting from the right, put a tick (✓) under the fifth bird.

4. Let's compare

Pupil Textbook pages 17–20

1. Which set has more? Which set has fewer? Put a
tick (✓) in the box next to the set that has more.

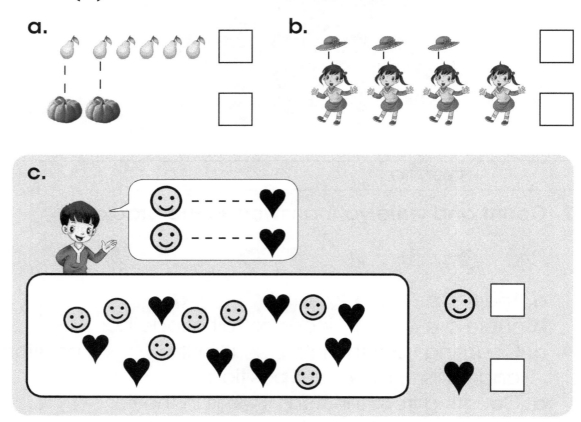

2. Write the numbers in the boxes, then write >, = or <
in the circles.

3. Write >, = or < in each ◯.

1 ◯ 3   2 ◯ 5   3 ◯ 6   0 ◯ 2

4 ◯ 1   5 ◯ 6   9 ◯ 9   3 ◯ 0

6 ◯ 7   3 ◯ 2   6 ◯ 6   0 ◯ 10

8 ◯ 8   4 ◯ 8   5 ◯ 10   5 ◯ 0

4. Draw the shapes to make the sentences true.

a. There are 2 fewer triangles than circles.

◯ ◯ ◯ ◯ ◯ ◯

_____

b. There are 3 more triangles than circles.

◯ ◯ ◯

_____

c. There are as many circles as squares.

▢ ▢ ▢ ▢

_____

d. There are 2 more squares than circles.

▢ ▢ ▢ ▢

_____

5. The number line

Pupil Textbook pages 21–22

1. Write the numbers in the boxes.

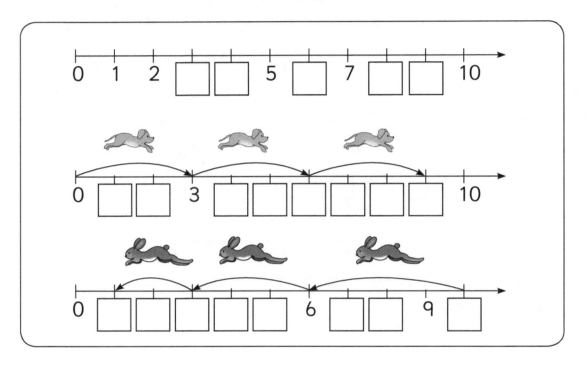

2. Compare. (Write >, = or < in each ◯.)

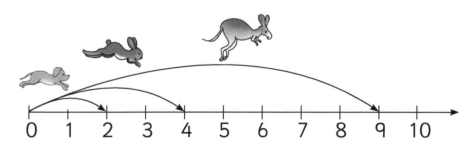

2 ◯ 4   9 ◯ 4   2 ◯ 9   0 ◯ 2

4 ◯ 2   4 ◯ 9   9 ◯ 2   4 ◯ 0

Unit Two: Addition and subtraction of numbers up to 10

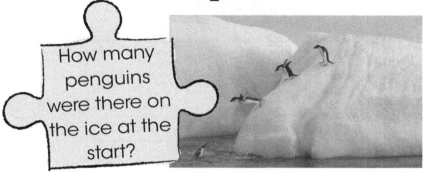

How many penguins were there on the ice at the start?

The table below lists the sections in this unit.

After completing each section, assess your work.

(Use 😊 if you are satisfied with your progress or 😐 if you are not satisfied.)

Section	Self-assessment
1. Number bonds	
2. Addition	
3. Describe and calculate (1)	
4. Subtract from	
5. Describe and calculate (2)	
6. Addition and subtraction	
7. Addition and subtraction using a number line	
8. Games about number 10	
9. Adding three numbers and subtracting two numbers	
10. Mixed addition and subtraction	

1. Number bonds

Pupil Textbook pages 24–25

1. Fill in the numbers to make 9.

9	
0	9
1	8
2	
3	
4	
5	
6	
7	
8	
9	

2. Guess the hidden numbers.

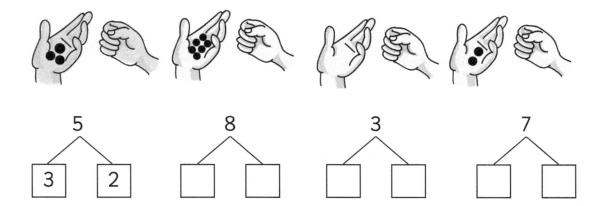

3. Write the correct numbers in the boxes.

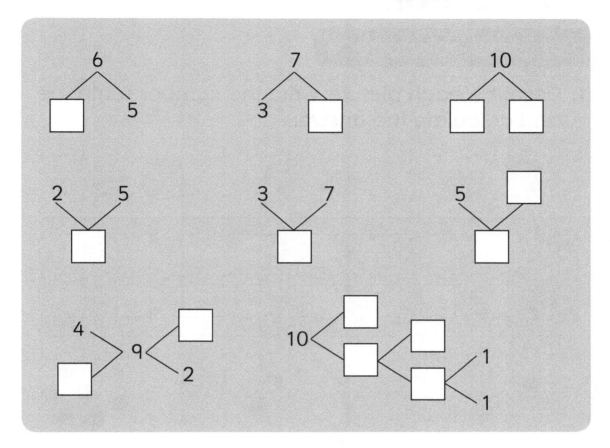

4. Draw lines to join pairs of numbers that make **10**.

2. Addition

Pupil Textbook page 26

1. Describe each picture, write the number sentence and calculate the answer.

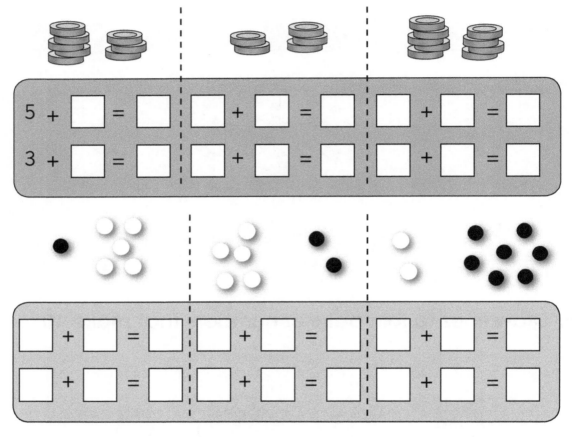

2. Link the number sentences where the addends have been exchanged, then calculate the answers.

3 + 7 = 10	3 + 6 =	6 + 2 =	8 + 2 =	1 + 0 =

2 + 8 =	2 + 6 =	6 + 3 =	0 + 1 =	7 + 3 =

1. How many dots are there altogether?

● ● ● ○ ○ ○ ○ ○ ○ ○

3   +   7 = ☐

● ● ● ● ● ○ ○ ○ ○ ○

5   +   ☐ = ☐

● ● ● ● ● ● ● ○ ○ ○ ○

☐ + ☐ = ☐

● ● ○ ○ ○ ○ ○ ○ ○ ○

☐ + ☐ = ☐

● ○ ○ ○ ○ ○ ○ ○ ○ ○

☐ + ☐ = ☐

○ ○ ○ ○ ○ ○ ○ ○ ○ ○

☐ + ☐ = ☐

2. Calculate.

3 + 4 =   7 + 1 =   2 + 3 =   7 + 0 =

5 + 1 =   2 + 4 =   2 + 2 =   4 + 6 =

0 + 5 =   4 + 4 =   7 + 3 =   3 + 6 =

3. Look at the picture, write the number sentences and calculate.

☐ + ☐ = ☐   ☐ + ☐ = ☐

☐ + ☐ = ☐   ☐ + ☐ = ☐

Pupil Textbook pages 28–29

1. Calculate.

$0 + 2 =$	$1 + 3 =$	$3 + 3 =$	$3 + 4 =$
$6 + 1 =$	$2 + 7 =$	$0 + 8 =$	$4 + 5 =$
$1 + 4 =$	$2 + 8 =$	$5 + 3 =$	$5 + 5 =$

2. Write the missing numbers in the boxes.

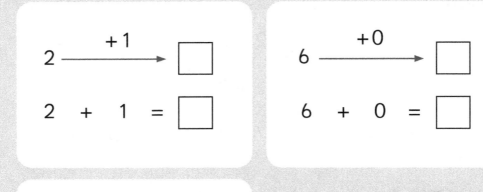

$2 \xrightarrow{+1} \square$

$2 + 1 = \square$

$6 \xrightarrow{+0} \square$

$6 + 0 = \square$

$7 \xrightarrow{+2} \square$

$7 + 2 = \square$

3. Describe each picture, write the number sentence and calculate the answer.

At the start there were 4 birds.

Another 3 birds arrived.

How many birds are there now?

At the start there were 2 tigers. Another 6 tigers arrived. How many tigers are there now?

3. Describe and calculate (1)

Pupil Textbook pages 30–31

1. Describe each picture, write the number
   sentence and calculate the answer.

a.

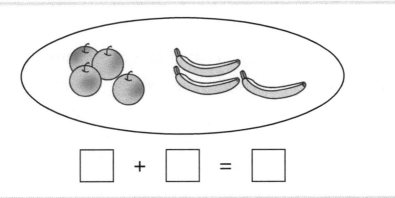

☐ + ☐ = ☐

b.

☐ + ☐ = ☐

c.

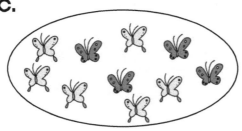

☐ + ☐ = ☐

☐ + ☐ = ☐

2. Calculate.

0 + 0 =	1 + 0 =	2 + 0 =	3 + 0 =
0 + 1 =	1 + 1 =	2 + 1 =	3 + 1 =
0 + 2 =	1 + 2 =	2 + 2 =	3 + 2 =
0 + 3 =	1 + 3 =	2 + 3 =	3 + 3 =
0 + 4 =	1 + 4 =	2 + 4 =	3 + 4 =
0 + 5 =	1 + 5 =	2 + 5 =	3 + 5 =
0 + 6 =	1 + 6 =	2 + 6 =	3 + 6 =
0 + 7 =	1 + 7 =	2 + 7 =	3 + 7 =
0 + 8 =	1 + 8 =	2 + 8 =	
0 + 9 =	1 + 9 =		
0 + 10 =			

4 + 0 =	5 + 0 =	6 + 0 =	7 + 0 =
4 + 1 =	5 + 1 =	6 + 1 =	7 + 1 =
4 + 2 =	5 + 2 =	6 + 2 =	7 + 2 =
4 + 3 =	5 + 3 =	6 + 3 =	7 + 3 =
4 + 4 =	5 + 4 =	6 + 4 =	
4 + 5 =	5 + 5 =		
4 + 6 =			

8 + 0 =	9 + 0 =	10 + 0 =
8 + 1 =	9 + 1 =	
8 + 2 =		

4. Subtract from

Pupil Textbook pages 32–34

1. Describe each picture, write the number sentence and calculate the answer.

At the start there were 9 tadpoles.

Then 3 tadpoles swam away.

How many tadpoles are left?

9 − ⬜ = ⬜

At the start there were 7 cakes.

Then 2 cakes were taken away.

How many cakes are left?

⬜ − ⬜ = ⬜

2. Fill in the missing numbers.

$3 \xrightarrow{\quad -1 \quad} \square$ $4 \xrightarrow{\quad -2 \quad} \square$ $4 \xrightarrow{\quad -1 \quad} \square$

$3 - 1 = \square$ $4 - 2 = \square$ $4 - 1 = \square$

$8 \xrightarrow{\quad -3 \quad} \square$ $9 \xrightarrow{\quad -4 \quad} \square$ $7 \xrightarrow{\quad -3 \quad} \square$

$8 - 3 = \square$ $9 - 4 = \square$ $7 - 3 = \square$

3. Calculate.

$10 - 1 =$ $9 - 3 =$ $7 - 6 =$ $8 - 5 =$

$6 - 2 =$ $10 - 4 =$ $8 - 2 =$ $8 - 8 =$

$9 - 7 =$ $6 - 3 =$ $7 - 4 =$ $5 - 4 =$

Pupil Textbook page 35

1. Describe each picture, write the number sentence and calculate the answer.

There are 7 rabbits in total. 4 rabbits are grey, and ____ rabbits are white.

There are 6 children. 3 of them are boys, and ____ of them are girls.

2. Read each question, write the number sentence and calculate the answer.

There are 5 ✏ and ✏ in total.	There are 5 🍐 and 🍎 altogther.
There are 2 ✏.	There are 4 🍐.
How many ✏ are there?	How many 🍎 are there?

☐ – ☐ = ☐   ☐ – ☐ = ☐

3. Fill in the missing numbers.

7 —[– 2]→ 5   4 —[–]→ 2   10 —[–]→ 2

8 —[–]→ 5   5 —[–]→ 3   6 —[–]→ 3

4. Calculate.

$0 - 0 =$	$2 - 0 =$	$3 - 0 =$	$4 - 0 =$
$1 - 0 =$	$2 - 1 =$	$3 - 1 =$	$4 - 1 =$
$1 - 1 =$	$2 - 2 =$	$3 - 2 =$	$4 - 2 =$
		$3 - 3 =$	$4 - 3 =$
			$4 - 4 =$
$8 - 0 =$	$7 - 0 =$	$6 - 0 =$	$5 - 0 =$
$8 - 1 =$	$7 - 1 =$	$6 - 1 =$	$5 - 1 =$
$8 - 2 =$	$7 - 2 =$	$6 - 2 =$	$5 - 2 =$
$8 - 3 =$	$7 - 3 =$	$6 - 3 =$	$5 - 3 =$
$8 - 4 =$	$7 - 4 =$	$6 - 4 =$	$5 - 4 =$
$8 - 5 =$	$7 - 5 =$	$6 - 5 =$	$5 - 5 =$
$8 - 6 =$	$7 - 6 =$	$6 - 6 =$	
$8 - 7 =$	$7 - 7 =$		
$8 - 8 =$			
$9 - 0 =$	$9 - 5 =$	$10 - 0 =$	$10 - 5 =$
$9 - 1 =$	$9 - 6 =$	$10 - 1 =$	$10 - 6 =$
$9 - 2 =$	$9 - 7 =$	$10 - 2 =$	$10 - 7 =$
$9 - 3 =$	$9 - 8 =$	$10 - 3 =$	$10 - 8 =$
$9 - 4 =$	$9 - 9 =$	$10 - 4 =$	$10 - 9 =$
			$10 - 10 =$

5. Describe and calculate (2)

Pupil Textbook pages 36–37

1. Describe each picture, write the number sentence and calculate the answer.

a.

⬜ – ⬜ = ⬜

b.

⬜ – ⬜ = ⬜

At the start there were
10 birds in the tree.

How many birds
were left in the tree?

☐ ◯ ☐ = ☐

At the start there were
10 birds in the tree.

How many birds
flew away?

☐ ◯ ☐ = ☐

2. Calculate and write the number sentences.

There are 6
altogether.

There are 4 baby .

How many adult 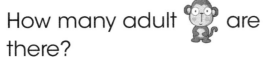 are
there?

☐ ◯ ☐ = ☐

There are 6
altogether.

There are 2 adult 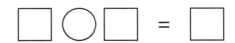 .

How many baby 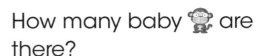 are
there?

☐ ◯ ☐ = ☐

3. Calculate.

10 − 5 =   5 − 4 =   10 − 6 =   2 − 1 =   10 − 3 =

6 − 3 =   3 − 0 =   8 − 4 =   0 − 0 =   10 − 2 =

6. Addition and subtraction

Pupil Textbook page 38

1. Fill in the missing numbers.

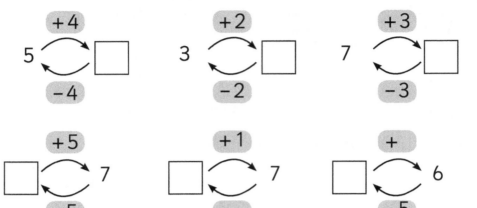

+4
5 ⟳ ☐
−4

+2
3 ⟳ ☐
−2

+3
7 ⟳ ☐
−3

+5
☐ ⟳ 7
−5

+1
☐ ⟳ 7
−

+
☐ ⟳ 6
−5

2. Fill in the missing numbers.

6 + 3 = ( )
9 − ( ) = ( )

3 + ( ) = 7
( ) − 3 = ( )

5 + ( ) = ( )
( ) − ( ) = ( )

3.

If ◯ + △ = ☆ , then ☆ − ( ) = ◯

7. Addition and subtraction using a number line

Pupil Textbook page 39

1. True or false? Put a tick (✓) for 'true' or a cross (✗) for 'false' in each ☐.

a.

+4

```
0   1   2   3   4   5   6   7   8   9
```

☐

The number sentence is 1 + 4 = 5

b.

+4

```
0   1   2   3   4   5   6   7   8   9
```

☐

The number sentence is 3 + 4 = 8

c.

+5

```
0   1   2   3   4   5   6   7   8   9
```

☐

The number sentence is 3 + 5 = 8

2. Fill in the missing numbers, calculate and write the number sentences.

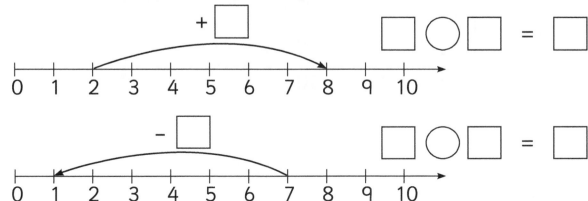

+ ☐

```
0   1   2   3   4   5   6   7   8   9   10
```

☐ ◯ ☐ = ☐

– ☐

```
0   1   2   3   4   5   6   7   8   9   10
```

☐ ◯ ☐ = ☐

8. Games about number 10

Pupil Textbook page 40

1. Calculate.

5 + 5 =	10 − 4 =	7 + 3 =	10 − 8 =
1 + 9 =	10 − 10 =	4 + 6 =	10 − 5 =
8 + 2 =	10 − 7 =	2 + 8 =	10 − 3 =

2. Fill in the missing numbers.

3 + ☐ = 10   10 = 2 + ☐

4 + ☐ = 10   10 = 7 + ☐

☐ + 5 = 10   10 = ☐ + 9

10 = ☐ + 0   ☐ + ☐ = 10

10 − ☐ = 3   10 − ☐ = 6

10 − ☐ = 5   10 − ☐ = 8

10 − ☐ = 1   10 − ☐ = 0

9. Adding three numbers and subtracting two numbers

Pupil Textbook page 41

1. Fill in the missing numbers.

a.

$6 - \boxed{} = 1$ $2 + \boxed{} = 7$ $\boxed{} + 8 = 8$

$\boxed{} + 5 = 9$ $\boxed{} - 4 = 5$ $10 - \boxed{} = 0$

$8 - \boxed{} = 3$ $\boxed{} + \boxed{} = 6$ $\boxed{} - \boxed{} = 2$

b.

$2 \xrightarrow{+1} \boxed{} \xrightarrow{+4} \boxed{}$ $3 \xrightarrow{+3} \boxed{} \xrightarrow{+2} \boxed{}$

$7 \xrightarrow{-3} \boxed{} \xrightarrow{-2} \boxed{}$ $10 \xrightarrow{-4} \boxed{} \xrightarrow{-5} \boxed{}$

2. Describe each picture, write the number sentence and calculate the answer.

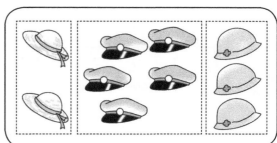

$3 + \boxed{} + \boxed{} = \boxed{}$ $\boxed{} + \boxed{} + \boxed{} = \boxed{}$

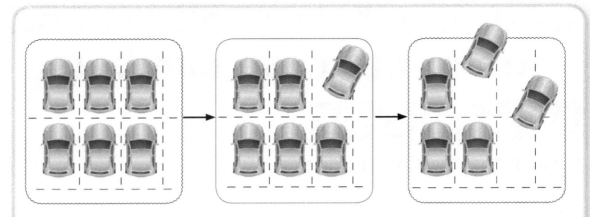

There were 6 cars. 1 car drove away. Then another 2 cars drove away. How many cars are left?

$$6 - \boxed{} - \boxed{} = \boxed{}$$

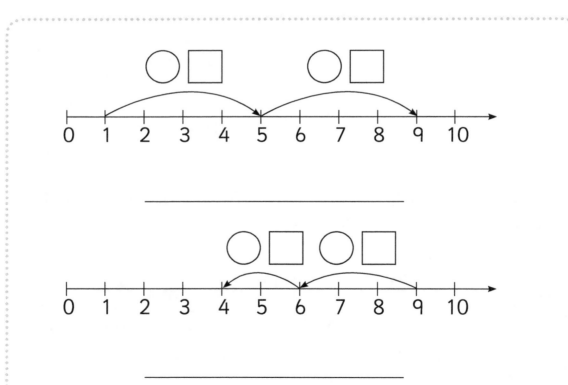

_____

_____

3. Calculate.

1 + 2 + 3 =   3 + 1 + 5 =   6 + 4 + 0 =

2 + 3 + 5 =   8 + 0 + 1 =   7 + 1 + 2 =

9 − 1 − 6 =   7 − 3 − 4 =   10 − 2 − 5 =

8 − 3 − 2 =   6 − 2 − 3 =   10 − 1 − 9 =

4. Draw lines to match the birds' cards to the nests.

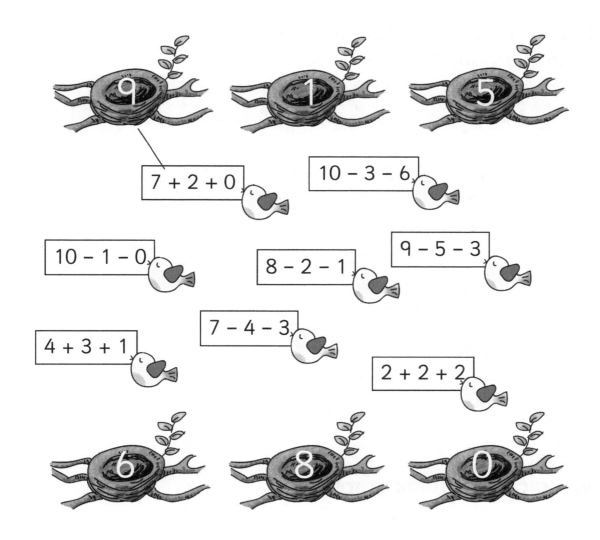

10. Mixed addition and subtraction

Pupil Textbook page 42

1. Fill in the missing numbers.

$3 \xrightarrow{+3} \square \xrightarrow{-2} \square$ $\qquad$ $9 \xrightarrow{-5} \square \xrightarrow{+1} \square$

$8 \xrightarrow{-4} \square \xrightarrow{+6} \square$ $\qquad$ $4 \xrightarrow{+3} \square \xrightarrow{-7} \square$

2. Describe each picture, write the number sentence and calculate the answer.

At the start there were 9 people on the bus.

3 people got off the bus and 2 people got on the bus.

How many people are there on the bus now?

$\square \bigcirc \square \bigcirc \square = \square$

3. Calculate.

$0 + 6 + 4 =$	$6 - 3 + 7 =$	$9 - 4 - 3 =$
$10 - 4 + 2 =$	$10 - 6 - 3 =$	$6 + 3 - 7 =$
$2 + 8 - 5 =$	$9 - 9 + 3 =$	$8 - 5 + 4 =$

4. Calculate. Think carefully.

$8 - 2 + 3 =$	$4 + 1 - 5 =$	$7 - 3 - 2 =$
$8 + 2 - 3 =$	$4 - 1 + 5 =$	$7 + 3 - 2 =$

Unit Three: Numbers from 0 to 20 and their addition and subtraction

There are ( ) 🦓 and ( ) 🦒.

There are ( ) 🦓 and 🦒 in total.

The table below lists the sections in this unit.

After completing each section, assess your work.

(Use 😊 if you are satisfied with your progress or 😐 if you are not satisfied.)

Section	Self-assessment
1. Numbers 11 to 20	
2. Tens and ones	
3. Ordering numbers up to 20	
4. Addition and subtraction	
5. Adding by making 10 first	
6. Describe and calculate (3)	
7. Adding and taking away	
8. The number wall	

3 Numbers from 0 to 20 and their addition and subtraction

1. Numbers 11 to 20

Pupil Textbook pages 44–45

1. Circle groups of 10, count and match.

a.

b.

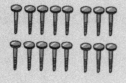   (16)

(17)

   (18)

(19)

(20)

2. Tens and ones

Pupil Textbook page 46

1. Describe each picture, write the number sentence and calculate the answer.

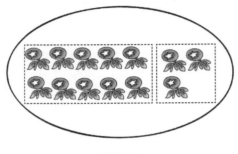
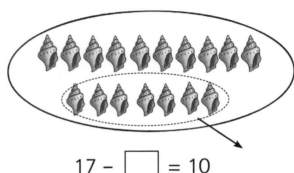

10 + ⬚ = 13   17 − ⬚ = 10

2. Calculate.

10 + 2 = ____	7 + 10 = ____	10 + 5 = ____
6 + 10 = ____	10 + 1 = ____	8 + 10 = ____
13 − 3 = ____	15 − 5 = ____	17 − 7 = ____
18 − 8 = ____	11 − 1 = ____	16 − 6 = ____

10 + 9 = ____	10 + 4 = ____	10 + 10 = ____
19 − 9 = ____	14 − 4 = ____	20 − 10 = ____
10 + ____ = 19	10 + ____ = 14	10 + ____ = 20
19 − ____ = 10	14 − ____ = 10	20 − ____ = 10

3. Write the numbers in the table.

12   17   14   20

Ten(s)	One(s)
1	2

4. Fill in the missing numbers.

a. One ten and three ones make (   ).

b. Five ones and one ten make (   ).

c. The ones digit is 7 and the tens digit is 1, so the number is (   ).

d. In the number 19, 9 is the (   ) digit, which means that (   ) is the (   ) digit.

In the number 20, 2 is the (   ) digit, which means that (   ) is the (   ) digit.

e. There are (   ) tens in 20, and there are (   ) ones in 20.

3. Ordering numbers up to 20

1. Count and match.

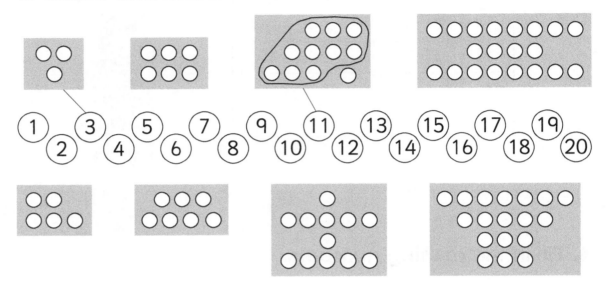

2. Join the points in the order of the numbers marked on the number line.

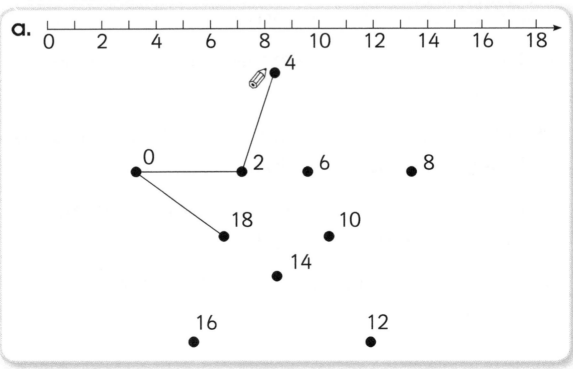

a.

b.

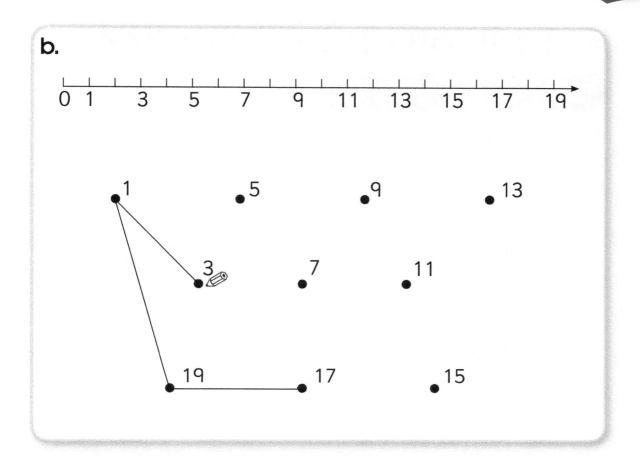

3. Write >, = or < in each ◯.

14 ◯ 18   20 ◯ 19   15 ◯ 11   13 ◯ 10   17 ◯ 18

16 ◯ 16   17 ◯ 15   15 ◯ 12   12 ◯ 20   20 ◯ 16

4. Addition and subtraction

Pupil Textbook page 48

1. Calculate.

$2 + 3 =$ _____ $6 + 2 =$ _____ $7 + 3 =$ _____

$12 + 3 =$ _____ $16 + 2 =$ _____ $17 + 3 =$ _____

$3 - 1 =$ _____ $5 - 3 =$ _____ $6 - 5 =$ _____

$13 - 1 =$ _____ $15 - 3 =$ _____ $16 - 5 =$ _____

2. Fill in the missing numbers. Follow the pattern to write the missing number sentences.

$3 + 4 =$ _____ $2 + 7 =$ _____ $4 + 6 =$ _____

$13 + 4 =$ _____   _____   _____

$4 - 2 =$ _____ $7 - 4 =$ _____ $9 - 8 =$ _____

$14 - 2 =$ _____   _____   _____

5. Adding by making 10 first

Pupil Textbook pages 49–50

1. Draw lines to join pairs of numbers in ⬤ and △ that make 10.

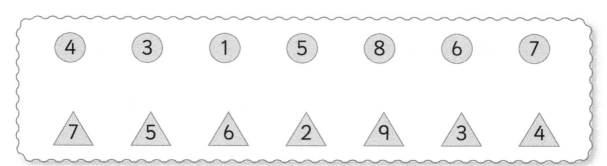

2. Fill in the missing numbers.

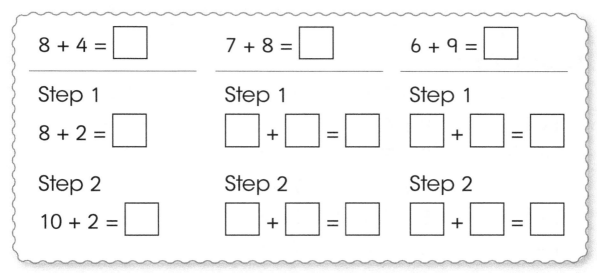

8 + 4 = ☐   7 + 8 = ☐   6 + 9 = ☐

Step 1
8 + 2 = ☐

Step 1
☐ + ☐ = ☐

Step 1
☐ + ☐ = ☐

Step 2
10 + 2 = ☐

Step 2
☐ + ☐ = ☐

Step 2
☐ + ☐ = ☐

3. Choose the correct number and put a tick (✓) in the brackets.

5 + 9 = { 15 (   )
          14 (   )
          13 (   )

8 + 3 = { 11 (   )
          12 (   )
          13 (   )

47

4. Calculate using your preferred method.

$3 + 9 =$ $7 + 7 =$ $6 + 8 =$ $5 + 6 =$

5. Describe each picture, write the number sentence and calculate the answer.

   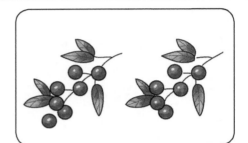

$5 + \boxed{} = \boxed{}$ $7 + \boxed{} = \boxed{}$

$8 + \boxed{} = \boxed{}$ $\boxed{} + \boxed{} = \boxed{}$

6. Calculate.

$9 + 2 =$	$8 + 3 =$	$7 + 4 =$	$6 + 5 =$
$9 + 3 =$	$8 + 4 =$	$7 + 5 =$	$6 + 6 =$
$9 + 4 =$	$8 + 5 =$	$7 + 6 =$	$6 + 7 =$
$9 + 5 =$	$8 + 6 =$	$7 + 7 =$	$6 + 8 =$
$9 + 6 =$	$8 + 7 =$	$7 + 8 =$	$6 + 9 =$
$9 + 7 =$	$8 + 8 =$	$7 + 9 =$	
$9 + 8 =$	$8 + 9 =$		
$9 + 9 =$			
$5 + 6 =$	$4 + 7 =$	$3 + 8 =$	$2 + 9 =$
$5 + 7 =$	$4 + 8 =$	$3 + 9 =$	
$5 + 8 =$	$4 + 9 =$		
$5 + 9 =$			

7. Describe each picture, write the number sentence and calculate the answer.

☐ + ☐ = ☐   ☐ + ☐ = ☐

8. Calculate.

10 + 2 =   6 + 11 =   3 + 8 =   8 + 4 =

7 + 6 =   7 + 9 =   2 + 13 =   8 + 7 =

9. Match pairs of numbers on the flowers that add to make the number on the vase.

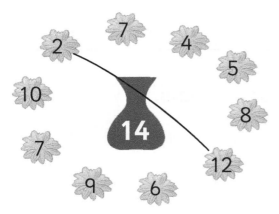 

10. Calculate and put each number sentence in the correct house.

6 + 8	9 + 7	5 + 9	7 + 7	6 + 9
7 + 8	12 + 3	8 + 8	3 + 12	10 + 6

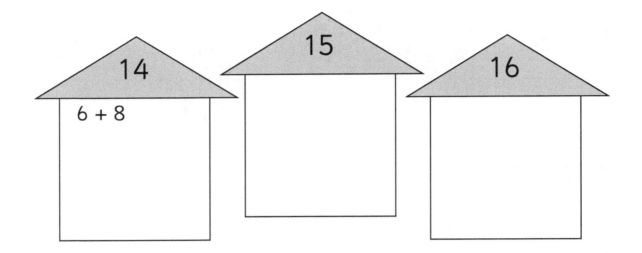

14

6 + 8

15

16

11. Fill in the missing numbers.

Addend	3	7	9	4	8	6	7
Addend	8	5	6	9	5	7	4
Sum	11						

12. Calculate. Think about your answers.

5 + 6 =	7 + 4 =	8 + 5 =
6 + 5 =	4 + 7 =	5 + 8 =

13. Describe each picture, write the number sentence and calculate the answer.

How many cups are there?

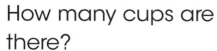

How many leaves are there?

At the start there were 7 fish.

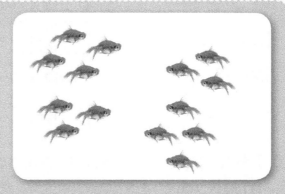

Another 7 fish arrived.

How many fish are there now?

1. Fill in the missing numbers.

$15 - 7 = \boxed{}$ $13 - 9 = \boxed{}$ $12 - 6 = \boxed{}$

Step 1   Step 1   Step 1

$15 - 5 = \boxed{}$ $\boxed{} - \boxed{} = \boxed{}$ $\boxed{} - \boxed{} = \boxed{}$

Step 2   Step 2   Step 2

$10 - 2 = \boxed{}$ $\boxed{} - \boxed{} = \boxed{}$ $\boxed{} - \boxed{} = \boxed{}$

2. Fill in the missing numbers.

$12 - 7 = \boxed{}$ $14 - 9 = \boxed{}$ $12 - 3 = \boxed{}$

Step 1   Step 1   Step 1

$10 - 7 = \boxed{}$ $\boxed{} - \boxed{} = \boxed{}$ $\boxed{} - \boxed{} = \boxed{}$

Step 2   Step 2   Step 2

$3 + 2 = \boxed{}$ $\boxed{} - \boxed{} = \boxed{}$ $\boxed{} - \boxed{} = \boxed{}$

3. Fill in the number sentences using your preferred method.

$11 - 5 = \boxed{}$

Step 1

_____

Step 2

_____

$20 - 4 = \boxed{}$

Step 1

_____

Step 2

_____

4. Calculate using your preferred method.

11 – 3 =   16 – 8 =   12 – 5 =   14 – 6 =

5. Calculate.

11 – 2 =   12 – 3 =   13 – 4 =   14 – 5 =

11 – 3 =   12 – 4 =   13 – 5 =   14 – 6 =

11 – 4 =   12 – 5 =   13 – 6 =   14 – 7 =

11 – 5 =   12 – 6 =   13 – 7 =   14 – 8 =

11 – 6 =   12 – 7 =   13 – 8 =   14 – 9 =

11 – 7 =   12 – 8 =   13 – 9 =

11 – 8 =   12 – 9 =

11 – 9 =

15 – 6 =   16 – 7 =   17 – 8 =   18 – 9 =

15 – 7 =   16 – 8 =   17 – 9 =

15 – 8 =   16 – 9 =

15 – 9 =

6. Describe each picture, write the number sentence and calculate the answer.

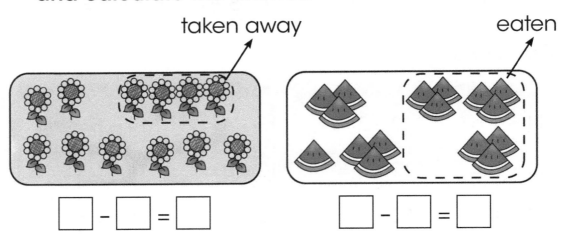

taken away   eaten

☐ – ☐ = ☐   ☐ – ☐ = ☐

7. Fill in the missing numbers.

11	☐
15	☐
13	– 8 = ☐
17	☐
14	☐

9	☐
5	☐
5 + 7	= ☐
10	☐
8	☐

12	☐
10	☐
16	– 7 = ☐
18	☐
15	☐

8. Calculate.

11 – 3 =	14 – 5 =	12 – 4 =	15 – 7 =
18 – 1 =	13 – 9 =	17 – 8 =	11 – 6 =
14 – 7 =	16 – 6 =	11 – 5 =	18 – 9 =
13 – 2 =	17 – 9 =	16 – 8 =	15 – 6 =
15 – 5 =	13 – 6 =	12 – 8 =	16 – 7 =

9. Fill in the missing numbers.

13 $\xrightarrow{\boxed{-5}}$ ☐ $\xrightarrow{\boxed{+4}}$ ☐ $\xrightarrow{\boxed{-2}}$ ☐ $\xrightarrow{\boxed{+9}}$ ☐

12 $\xrightarrow{\boxed{+6}}$ ☐ $\xrightarrow{\boxed{-9}}$ ☐ $\xrightarrow{\boxed{+10}}$ ☐ $\xrightarrow{\boxed{-7}}$ ☐

10. Describe each picture, write the number sentence and calculate the answer.

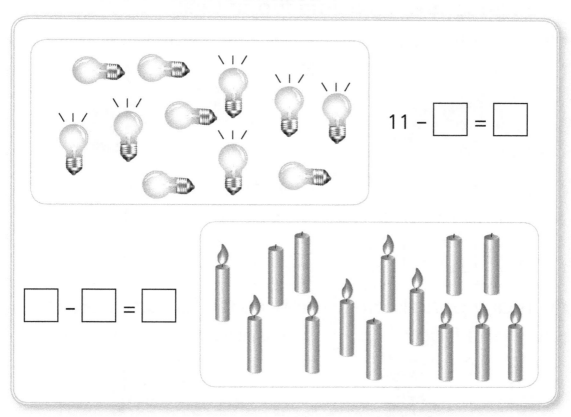

$11 - \boxed{} = \boxed{}$

$\boxed{} - \boxed{} = \boxed{}$

11. Match the calculations with the same answers.

13 – 6	15 – 9		17 – 10	11 – 8
11 – 5	11 – 4		12 – 9	15 – 7
18 – 8	12 – 2		13 – 5	14 – 7

12. Fill in the missing numbers.

7 + (   ) = 11   9 + (   ) = 16   3 + (   ) = 12

11 – 7 = (   )   16 – (   ) = (   )   (   ) – 3 = (   )

13. Describe each picture, write the number sentence and calculate the answer.

At the start there were 11 children.

How many children were left on the bus?

☐ ◯ ☐ = ☐

There are 13 vegetables in total.

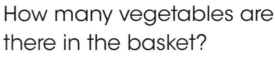

How many vegetables are there in the basket?

☐ ◯ ☐ = ☐

How many pencils are there in the bag?

There are 12 pencils in total.

☐ ◯ ☐ = ☐

How many fish are there in the fishbowl behind the cat?

There are 11 fish in total.

☐ ◯ ☐ = ☐

6. Describe and calculate (3)

Pupil Textbook pages 53–54

1. Describe each picture, write the number sentence and calculate the answer.

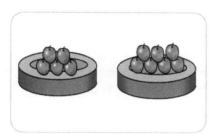

How many apples are there in total?

How many birds flew away?

□ ○ □ = □

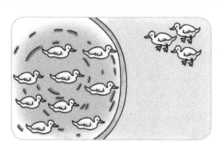

How many ducks are there in total?

□ ○ □ = □

There are 15 carrots in total.

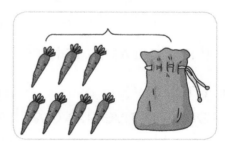

How many carrots are there in the sack?

□ ○ □ = □

2. Make up questions and write the number sentences.

a. There were 16 children on , and then 7 children got off. _____

b. There were 8 children on , and then another 6 children got on. _____

c. There are 10 children on and 7 children on . _____

d. There are 15 children in total on two buses, and there are 9 children on . _____

e. There were 4 children on , and then some more children got on. Then there were 13 children on . _____

3. Write number sentences and calculate the answers.

a. has 10 , has as many as . How many do they have in total?

b. There were 8 . Some more birds arrived. Now there are 12 . How many have arrived?

c. There were some on the river. After 9 ducks swam away, 5 ducks were left. How many were there on the river at the start?

7. Adding and taking away

Pupil Textbook page 55

1. Describe each picture, write the number sentence and calculate the answer.

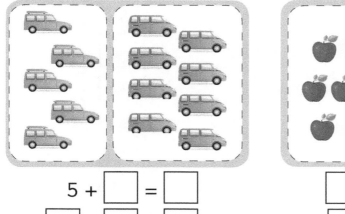

$5 +$ ☐ $=$ ☐

☐ $-$ ☐ $=$ ☐

☐ $+$ ☐ $=$ ☐

☐ $-$ ☐ $=$ ☐

2. Fill in the missing numbers.

$9 + 7 =$ ☐ $11 - 3 =$ ☐ $6 + 6 =$ ☐ $12 - 7 =$ ☐

$16 - 9 =$ ☐ $3 + 8 =$ ☐   ☐ $-$ ☐ $=$ ☐   ☐ $+$ ☐ $=$ ☐

3. Make up questions and write the number sentences.

a. At the start there were 11 🐯 playing on the grass. Now 4 of them have gone back home.

_____

b. Dylan has 7 🐟 . His father bought another 4.

_____

59

8. The number wall

Pupil Textbook page 56

1. Complete these number walls.

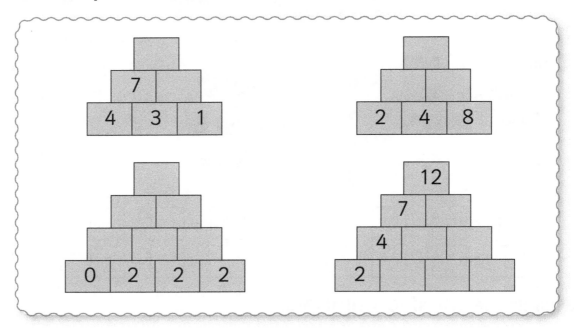

2. Complete these number walls.

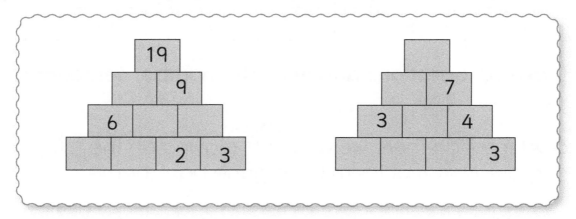

Unit Four: Recognising shapes

Find objects at home that have these shapes.

Then find objects that have these shapes.

The table below lists the sections in this unit.

After completing each section, assess your work.

(Use 😊 if you are satisfied with your progress or 😐 if you are not satisfied.)

Section	Self-assessment
1. Shapes of objects	

1. Shapes of objects

Pupil Textbook pages 58–60

1. Match the shapes.

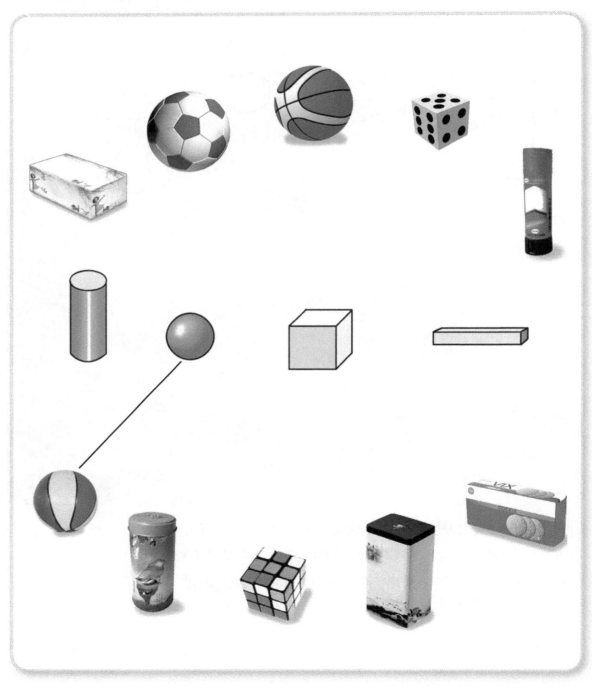

2. Count the shapes and complete the table.

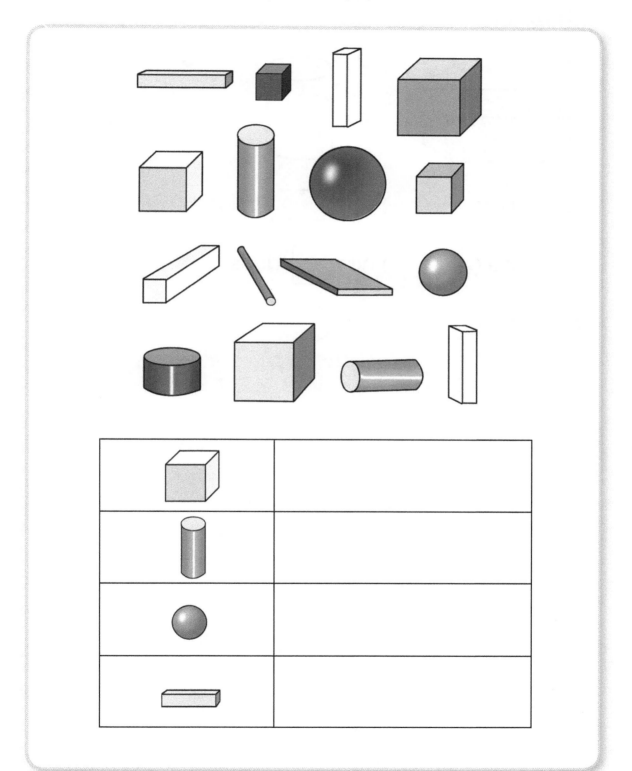

3. Write the number of the correct shape in the brackets.

1.

2.

3.

a. Shape (   ) has [   ] faces.

b. Shape (   ) has [   ] faces.

c. Shape (   ) has ( ) faces.

Unit Five: Consolidating and enhancing

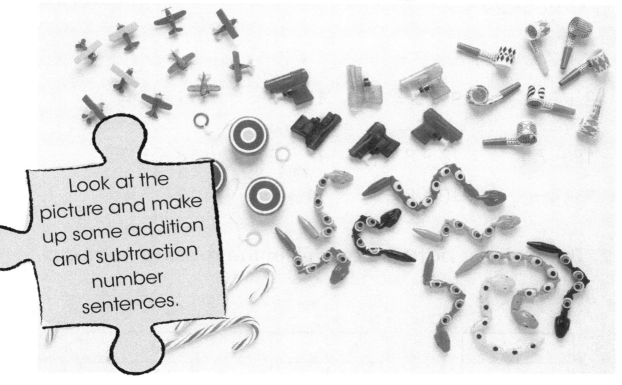

Look at the picture and make up some addition and subtraction number sentences.

The table below lists the sections in this unit.

After completing each section, assess your work.

(Use 😊 if you are satisfied with your progress or 😐 if you are not satisfied.)

Section	Self-assessment
1. Calculations	
2. Comparing numbers	
3. Double and halve	
4. Let's do addition	
5. Let's do subtraction	
6. Writing number sentences	

1. Calculations

Pupil Textbook page 63

1. Calculate.

2 + 7 =	3 + 7 =	4 + 7 =	5 + 7 =
8 + 5 =	9 + 5 =	10 + 5 =	11 + 5 =

18 – 7 =	18 – 8 =	18 – 9 =	18 – 10 =
9 – 4 =	10 – 5 =	11 – 6 =	12 – 7 =

2. Think about patterns and fill in the missing numbers.

+ 2	
9	
10	
11	
12	
13	

+ 6	
4	
5	
6	
7	

+ 8	
12	
11	
10	
9	

– 5	
7	
8	
9	
10	
11	

– 7	
8	
9	
10	
11	

– 8	
19	
18	
17	
16	

2. Comparing numbers

Pupil Textbook pages 64–65

1. Look at the pictures and compare the numbers.

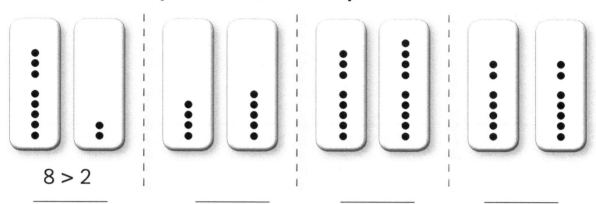

8 > 2 _____   _____   _____   _____

2. Write >, = or < in each ◯.

5 ◯ 6   7 ◯ 4   16 ◯ 16   20 ◯ 2

3. Write >, = or < in each ◯.

10 + 7 ◯ 10   13 ◯ 7 + 6   6 + 12 ◯ 8

20 ◯ 1 + 19   11 – 2 ◯ 11   8 – 4 ◯ 4

15 – 5 ◯ 5   16 – 6 ◯ 16

4. Write >, = or < in each ◯.

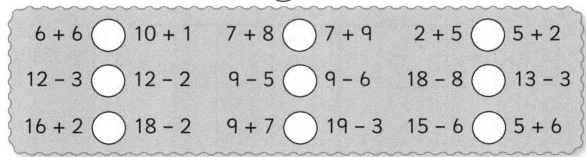

6 + 6 ◯ 10 + 1   7 + 8 ◯ 7 + 9   2 + 5 ◯ 5 + 2

12 – 3 ◯ 12 – 2   9 – 5 ◯ 9 – 6   18 – 8 ◯ 13 – 3

16 + 2 ◯ 18 – 2   9 + 7 ◯ 19 – 3   15 – 6 ◯ 5 + 6

3. Double and halve

Pupil Textbook page 66

1. Count the dots and draw the matching pattern above the line.

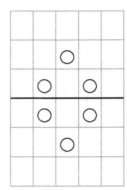 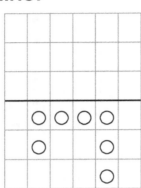 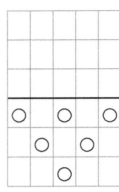 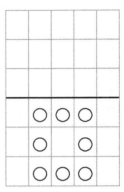

2. Draw dots and fill in the numbers.

2	○○	○○ ─── ○○	2 + 2	4
4		───────		
5		───────		
7		───────		

3. Fill in the missing numbers.

Doubling ↓

1	2		5	6	7			10
2	4	8				16	18	

↑ Halving

4. Fill in the missing numbers.

The number of balloons I have is double 5, which is (   ).

The number of balloons I have is double the result of double 2, which is (   ).

The number of balloons I have is double the number monkey has. I have (   ) balloons.

The number of balloons I have is half the number dog has. I have (   ) balloons.

4. Let's do addition

Pupil Textbook page 67

1. Write suitable numbers in the boxes.

☐ + ☐ = ☐ + ☐ = ☐ + ☐ = ☐ + ☐ = 10

☐ + ☐ = ☐ + ☐ = ☐ + ☐ = ☐ + ☐ = 15

2. Find the pattern to fill in the missing number sentences. Then calculate the answers.

6 + 3		8 + 3
		8 + 4
6 + 5		

7 + 4	8 + 4
7 + 5	8 + 5

6 + 6	
5 + 7	

5. Let's do subtraction

Pupil Textbook page 68

1. Write suitable numbers in the boxes.

$$\boxed{} - \boxed{} = \boxed{} - \boxed{} = \boxed{} - \boxed{} = \boxed{} - \boxed{} = 5$$

$$\boxed{} - \boxed{} = \boxed{} - \boxed{} = \boxed{} - \boxed{} = \boxed{} - \boxed{} = 9$$

2. Find the pattern to fill in the missing number sentences. Then calculate the answers.

11 – 3		13 – 3
		14 – 4
13 – 5		

13 – 7

	14 – 8	15 – 8	

6. Writing number sentences

Pupil Textbook page 69

1. Fill in the missing numbers.

7 + 8 = ☐   10 + 2 = ☐   6 + 11 = ☐   9 + 5 = ☐

8 + 7 = ☐   2 + 10 = ☐   11 + 6 = ☐   5 + 9 = ☐

15 − 7 = ☐   12 − 2 = ☐   17 − 6 = ☐   14 − 5 = ☐

15 − 8 = ☐   12 − 10 = ☐   17 − 11 = ☐   14 − 9 = ☐

2. Look at the pictures and write suitable number sentences.

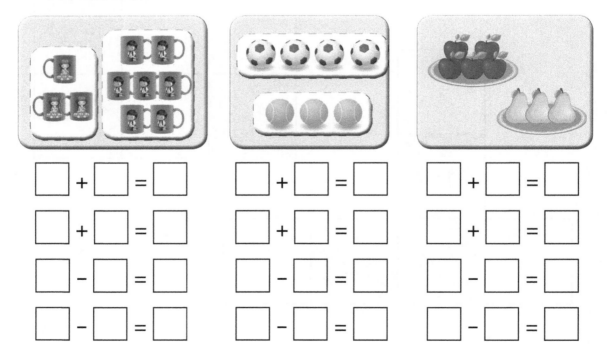

☐ + ☐ = ☐   ☐ + ☐ = ☐   ☐ + ☐ = ☐

☐ + ☐ = ☐   ☐ + ☐ = ☐   ☐ + ☐ = ☐

☐ − ☐ = ☐   ☐ − ☐ = ☐   ☐ − ☐ = ☐

☐ − ☐ = ☐   ☐ − ☐ = ☐   ☐ − ☐ = ☐

3. Choose three of the numbers given below and use them to write two addition sentences and two subtraction sentences. Write at least three groups of number sentences.

20	9	14	6	7	16	15	8

_____ _____ _____ _____

_____ _____ _____ _____

_____ _____ _____ _____

_____ _____ _____ _____

4. Look at the pictures and write two addition sentences and two subtraction sentences. Complete the calculations.

_____ _____

_____ _____

Appendix 1 Writing numerals

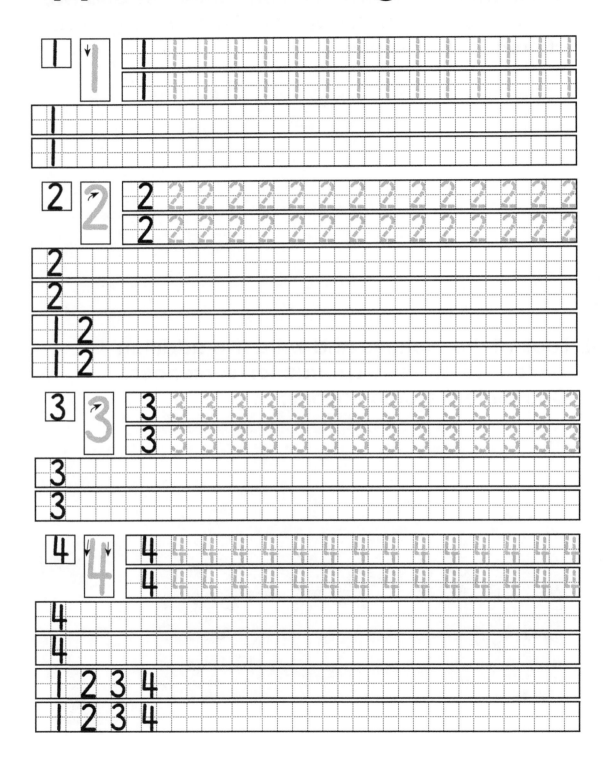

5 5 5 5 5 5 5 5 5 5 5 5 5 5 5 5 5

5 5 5 5 5 5 5 5 5 5 5 5 5 5 5 5 5

5

5

0 0 0 0 0 0 0 0 0 0 0 0 0 0 0 0 0 0

0 0 0 0 0 0 0 0 0 0 0 0 0 0 0 0 0 0

0

0

4 5 0

4 5 0

6 6 6 6 6 6 6 6 6 6 6 6 6 6 6 6

6 6 6 6 6 6 6 6 6 6 6 6 6 6 6 6

6

6

7 7 7 7 7 7 7 7 7 7 7 7 7 7 7 7

7 7 7 7 7 7 7 7 7 7 7 7 7 7 7 7

7

7

5 6 7

5 6 7

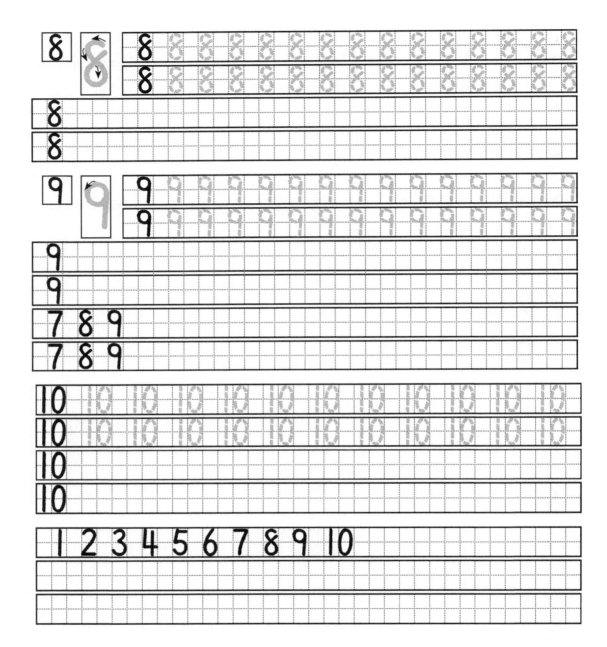

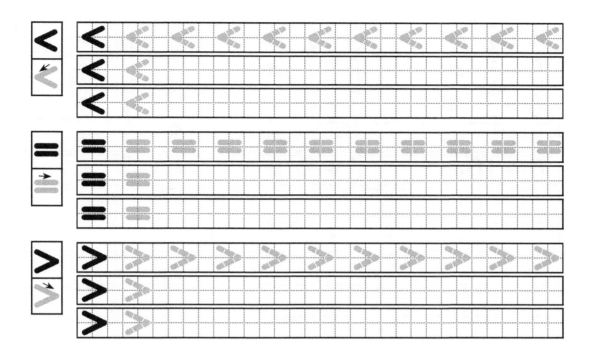

Appendix 2 Writing additions

1 + 2 =	3 + 2 =	2 + 0 =
5 + 3 =	8 + 1 =	3 + 3 =
6 + 2 =	3 + 4 =	2 + 7 =
4 + 4 =	2 + 5 =	8 + 2 =
0 + 10 =	6 + 3 =	4 + 2 =

9 + 2 =	7 + 8 =	3 + 8 =
8 + 5 =	6 + 6 =	8 + 9 =
6 + 7 =	7 + 9 =	8 + 6 =
4 + 9 =	8 + 8 =	6 + 5 =
7 + 7 =	4 + 8 =	9 + 6 =
9 + 5 =	5 + 7 =	9 + 9 =

Appendix 3 Writing subtractions

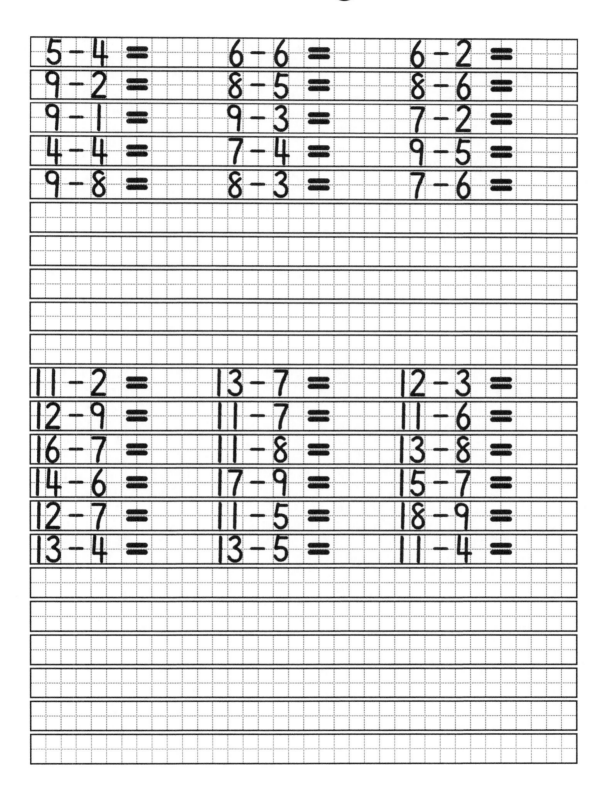

5 - 4 =	6 - 6 =	6 - 2 =
9 - 2 =	8 - 5 =	8 - 6 =
9 - 1 =	9 - 3 =	7 - 2 =
4 - 4 =	7 - 4 =	9 - 5 =
9 - 8 =	8 - 3 =	7 - 6 =

11 - 2 =	13 - 7 =	12 - 3 =
12 - 9 =	11 - 7 =	11 - 6 =
16 - 7 =	11 - 8 =	13 - 8 =
14 - 6 =	17 - 9 =	15 - 7 =
12 - 7 =	11 - 5 =	18 - 9 =
13 - 4 =	13 - 5 =	11 - 4 =